Dream Manual

_____

For Therapists and Other Listeners

Dream Manual

For Therapists and Other Listeners

Galen Martini, MA, LP
Licensed Psychologist/Jungian Analyst

NORTH STAR PRESS OF ST. CLOUD, INC.
St. Cloud, Minnesota

Cover Painting: Gina M. Baird
Cover Design: Jennifer Morrissette-Hesse

Copyright © 2011 Galen Martini, OSB

ISBN: 0-87839-562-8
ISBN-13: 978-0-87839-562-0

First Edition, May 2011

Printed in the United States of America

Published by
North Star Press of St. Cloud, Inc.
P.O. Box 451
St. Cloud, Minnesota 56302

www.northstarpress.com

Dedication

This book is dedicated to the memory of two great Minnesota Jungian analysts: Chris Santella, my beloved training analyst who burst upon heaven unexpectedly between one analytic session and another. She is still greatly missed. And Mary Ann Mattoon, whose many books translate Jung's writings into clear and understandable prose. She has been a good friend and an inspiration. This little manual on dreams is following in her large footsteps.

Acknowledgements

I am most grateful to my dear friends, colleagues, workshop participants and clients who encouraged the writing of this book by asking me questions, working on their own dreams, and for some, reading the manuscript in its earlier forms. Many thanks especially to Annette Brophy, OSB, Mara Faulkner, OSB, and Katherine Howard, OSB, for their many kindnesses and helps over the years, and to friends and fellow Jungians Dr. Claudia Johnson, Karen Magee and Dr. Jennette Jones, whose love and encouragement kept the idea of this book afloat. To my sisters Dee Edelbrock and Mona Moeller, a big thank you for hearing my oft told tale "my book is coming soon," with patience and belief, for yes, here indeed it is!

Thank you, too, to all the Minnesota Jungian analysts who have been my analyst, mentors, supervising analysts, teachers and friends through the long and rigorous studies that make up Jungian analyst training. Your words are not forgotten.

Olivia Forster, OSB, proofread the manuscript most carefully and Susan Sink answered many questions and helped me transfer words to computerese. My niece, artist and art therapist, Gina Baird, created the whimsical cover painting, and Jennifer Morrissette Hesse designed it into a lovely cover. Editors Corinne and Seal Dwyer of North Star Press helped me bring this dream of a *Dream Manual* to life. Many thanks to all!

About the Author

Galen Martini is a Jungian Psychoanalyst and Licensed Psychologist in private practice, who specializes in working with dreams and art as ways of accessing the unconscious. She has been doing clinical work for some twenty-five years, teaching workshops on Jungian topics at the local and national level, and consulting with therapists and others in the listening professions who are learning to use dreams in their own practice. Galen is a prize-winning poet, winner of the Bush Foundation Fellowship for Artists and the Loft Mentor Award. She has a published book of poems and phtographs, *The Heart's Slow Race: A Farewell to the Land*, a monograph on Jung's individuation, *Finding Your Own Life*, as well as numerous articles, essays, reviews, and multimedia scripts and photographs. She is a mixed-media artist, exploring visual journals, altered books, and left-handed paintings for their messages from the guiding psyche. Galen is a member of Saint Benedict's Monastery in St. Joseph, Minnesota.

Table of Contents

Introduction

WHETHER YOU ARE A THERAPIST, psychologist, pastoral or school counselor, hospital chaplain, life coach, or spiritual director, you will, from time to time, be given the role of dream interpreter, "ready or not." More and more people are discovering their dreams as meaningful, and expect the guides with whom they work to help them decipher their meaning. Perhaps you have already been asked to comment on clients' dreams for help on a current situation. Or you have been asked to help someone trying to make an important decision. When she brings you a dream, you may not know how to let the dream shed light on the situation.

If you are a therapist, perhaps you have wished there were a way to wake up a client to some insight he desperately needs but simply can't see. You know that, if you simply tell him, the ideas seem foreign to him, his defenses kick in and begin to sabotage the progress you have made. Or perhaps you have a client who comes in session after session with reportage of what happened during the week, but who cannot see where she is repeating self-defeating patterns learned early in life with her boss, work colleagues, or husband. You may have wondered how to break through the scramble of details to get to the heart of the matter.

Then the breakthrough happens. This same person comes to a session shaken by a dream she knows is important. She drops the pattern of reporting repetitious facts and tells you the story of the dream. She waits for you to comment. You know there is something big happening here. This is the teaching moment for which you have been waiting. But the dream is confusing, the images powerful but strange. It's as if they are in a foreign language. You know you need to respond. Would you know how to proceed?

This dreamwork manual is designed for the practitioner who, though trained in his or her specialty, has had no classes along the way in working with the powerful unconscious, in interpreting dreams. Though we all have had the experience of being completely transfixed by a dream ourselves, the skills of working with dreams have mostly been confined to the long and rigorous training of Jungian and Freudian psychoanalysts.

Yet there is an innate sense of how important the dream world is. And this is part of our common heritage. Even a cursory study of dreams shows an ancestry of dream interpretation that stretches back through virtually all ancient cultures. The experience and power of dreams is such a part of our heritage as human beings that we can hardly fathom a time when people have not awakened from a dream and known they were being touched in some way by a power beyond themselves. The Christian scriptures, all the major world religions, and all world civilizations have had belief in and respect for dreams as a welling up and breaking through of wisdom from a place deeper than the conscious human mind can contrive or understand.

In our own time, scientists have done their studies, discovering what is happening in sleep, reporting that in REM (rapid eye movement) sleep we all dream in ninety-minute cycles through the night, for a total of roughly an hour and a half of dream-time per night. Deprived of REM dreaming sleep, people rapidly become irritable, disorganized, even disoriented. Dreams have been studied by scientists and scholars, psychoanalysts and religions, and now have reached millions via popular books and articles, regular newspaper columns, and Internet sites.

Various approaches have been used, some of them evocative and helpful, others excessively popularized and reductive, making of deep and individual dream symbols trite one-to-one arbitrary meanings—"If you dream of rings, your romantic partner is about to find you." Yet we all know that our psyches are a rich source of ideas and images that create a new story or screenplay every single night, and several times every night. And the meanings come from our individual world of experiences, associations, and symbols.

Far beyond any dream dictionary, these symbols have been living and forming in us since our birth and, according to Carl Jung, even before our birth. Human nature has been storing meanings for as long as human beings have been around. He called this the "collective unconscious," the long millions of years' memory we all carry as part of the human race. So when we are fearful or caught in a hard bind, abusive relationship, or difficult decision, our dreams use some of the same stories that have resonated down through the centuries. Serious students of dreams like to read these stories and deep myths to see the resonances with dream themes of their own.

As you undertake this study of dreams, know that you can find books and articles to help you in any aspect of dream work, from the archetypal to the immediately helpful and practical. I have geared this dream manual to the working practitioner using an eclectic approach, but one grounded in the depth psychology of Carl Jung.

Despite the fact that we live in times and belief systems very different from our ancient ancestors, dreams continue to fascinate us with their relevance to our daily lives. They offer us insights on the conflicts and anxieties that concern us, and help heal the splits within us between our over-socialized selves and the worlds we carry within. All of us are more than our outer world attests to, or the faces we have to wear for our roles in the world. Dreams help us stay in touch with our "more than meets the eye" Self we carry within.

"In each of us there is another whom we do not know. He speaks to us in dreams and tells us how differently he sees us from the way we see ourselves. When, therefore, we find ourselves in a difficult situation in which there is no solution, he can sometimes kindle a light that radically alters our attitude—the very attitude that led us into the difficult situation."

(C.G. Jung CW 10, par. 325)

Chapter 1

The Therapist Meets the Dream

HAT DO DREAMS DO for the working therapist who wants to help his/her patients or clients find their way out of the problems which beset them and into a clearer, more productive, happier life? In this and the next chapters, we will look at some dream work basics, beginning with how to help ourselves and our clients remember dreams. It will help if you, too, become a student of your own dreams. It is amazing the insight you will begin to pick up about yourself, but also at times about the relationships between you and your clients. This can offer you great help in difficult situations.

We'll explore how to begin to learn the language of dreams by looking at what dreams do, how dreams are structured, how to write them down and work with them to find their meanings, what functions different kinds of dreams serve, how they help you in your work with clients, and what insights they are offering you in specific situations.

For example the "initial dream" is the dream which normally comes early in your work with a new patient, in which the work ahead of you is laid out for you in symbolic terms. The dreamer's task (and yours) could be depicted as a "difficult climb," "uphill against a wind," "like driving down an unknown street in a fog." Or is the client "just climbing out of a deep hole," "having his house reconstructed," or "getting into a new car" and a new way of moving in the world? In any case, it is helpful for you to be tipped off by the client's own psyche as to the nature of the work ahead.

And how does the client's psyche view this work and you the therapist? What do you look like to the patient's psyche? Does a helper figure of some sort show up in her dream and, if so, on whom are you modeled? Are you being cast in the guise of a feared father or an interfering mother? All of these are feelings your patient may not know or be able to voice if she does. And most certainly the way he or she unconsciously views you will affect the quality of your therapeutic alliance. We will talk further about transference/countertransference issues and how the dream can help, in a further chapter.

For now let's take a look at some of the things dreams do:

1. Dreams help the dreamer know what she is really feeling—especially when that is different from what she thinks she is supposed to feel. (We've all been socialized to the point where we often can't tell the difference.)
2. Dreams show needs that are habitually going unnoticed or are even actively being demeaned or disowned by the dreamer's current attitude or learned value system.
3. Dreams show outdated versions of the dreamer he is still trying to keep alive—often revealing the conflict and the cost of the struggle.
4. Dreams will sometimes reveal what habitually goes wrong in a problematic set of encounters—the "anatomy of a complex." These are the kinds of personal conundrums that can

take years to "figure out," and the dream suddenly makes them clear.

5. Dreams kindly show us the self-defeating patterns that used to work, and how they work now. Sometimes they reveal their origin.

6. Dreams tell the dreamer "the rest of the story." For example, revealing why such strong feelings are engendered by some innocuous person at work, or why the dreamer starts to avoid the new job she worked so hard to get. The code persons the dream uses, or the way the dream depicts the place, can show what story from the past is going on beneath the surface. (Example: "Coworker in dream looks like Uncle Mike who abused me.")

7. Dreams can fill in the blanks—showing the dreamer what he or she may have noticed peripherally and doesn't really know she knows. It may surround her with the "flavor" of a place that is affecting her unconsciously, and answer the question "Why do I love this place, or why do I hate it so much?"

8. Dreams compensate for one-sided attitudes with a broader view. For example, when depressed, people cannot "think straight." Yet their dreams can model an attitude that is "the way out of the woods." It is as if, in the dream, the client's real potential is being acted out, giving the dreamer a chance to feel the new energy which could come with some needed change.

9. In fact, dreams reveal shadow aspects of the dreamer. Not only the dark side, or hidden cruelties we think or act out on others, but also the unconscious ways we demean ourselves Sometimes the dream makes clear the ways the dreamer has been taught to belittle aspects of himself. These

can show up in the dream as people of the same sex who carry talents he himself has buried or been taught to ignore, and now the dream brings news of this potential.

10. Dreams show options the dreamer may not have thought of until now. Some person, place, or event in the dream can kindle a new plan or career choice, or wake a passion for what one has denied or put away for too long.

11. Dreams are creative sources of energy for the new way—not only revealing what could be, but giving the jolt of energy to start moving in that direction.

For all these reasons, dreams are a great source of help to both the client and the therapist. Now there is help actively given from within the patient who seeks your guidance. Rather than having to rely on your own store of good advice, adapting it to this client, the psyche is tailor-making advice and handing it to both of you through dream messages. What remains then is learning to decode these messages and learning to trust your ability to connect with your own and your client's inherent wisdom.

Chapter One Points to Remember:
The Therapist Meets the Dream

- Because dreams are coming from a place of which your client is "unconscious" (from "the unconscious"), dreams supply a fund of rich information which augments the personal story or presenting problem the client brings.
- An "initial dream," for example, coming as it does in the first couple of sessions, can act as a kind of setting the stage for the coming work. It can be used as a metaphor for the work ahead, and even as a prognostic tool.
- Dreams of caretakers or authority figures, teachers, doctors, therapists can show you what habitual attitudes your client carries and which might be helpful or difficult in your work with this client. In any case, you are getting an added help as the dream shows in whose shoes you are now standing. Transference dreams such as this show what feelings are being transferred from an earlier time into this therapeutic work with you.
- Likewise your own dreams can reveal how you feel about your client (your countertransference). Remember the dream is a metaphor and is using symbolic language: however it can reveal your own projections and feelings transferred from another time and place onto this client.
- Don't be afraid to get an hour or two of supervision where you sense transference or countertransference feelings are getting in the way of doing good work.
- In short, dreams do many things to compensate or reveal the present situation. They show us "the rest of the story."

"Dreams are impartial, spontaneous products of the unconscious psyche, outside the control of the will. They are pure nature; they show us the unvarnished natural truth, and are therefore fitted, as nothing else is, to give us back an attitude that accords with our basic human nature when our consciousness has strayed too far from its foundations and run into an impasse."

(C.G. Jung, CW 10, par. 317)

Chapter 2

Getting Started with Your Own Dreams

OW DO YOU BEGIN TO HELP CLIENTS, patients, directees, counselees with the dreams they bring you? How do you move to the world of dreams with some authority? The first step is learning to listen to your own dreams. Without some personal experience of your own dream life and dream language, your work will be theoretical and superficial, and you will easily run out of ideas for helping your clients find their dreams meaningful.

Some Steps for Beginning to Listen to Your Dreams

- Have a pad and paper near your bed, or wherever you would be able to jot down the dream when you wake.
- Morning is the best time for catching a dream, but anytime you wake up with one, you can jot down as much as you can before returning to sleep.
- In the morning, let yourself wake up slowly if you can, and mull over the dream before jumping up. Fast movement can destroy dream memory. Write it down as soon as you

can, even if only a brief few words or brief sketch of the plot line. Even if the dream seems so vivid you think you'll never forget it, you will lose the small details that give invaluable clues to its meaning.

- Remember scientists assure us that everyone dreams through the night. However, learning to remember, record, and discover the dream's meaning is a skill that, like any other sport or art form, improves with practice.

- Write down everything you remember as quickly as you can, and don't let yourself censor as to content or "craziness." Every detail is unique to this dream and taken together provides the "textual clues" to its meaning.

- Have a dream notebook specifically for dreams, or include dreams with the rest of your daily musings in your journal.

- After you have several dreams recorded, find a time when you can spend half an hour or hour on a dream that feels like it stands out, or has special interest for you. You will find that, while some dreams lend themselves to mulling through the day, there are always a couple that call to you for more detailed study. You will find that every time you sit down to explore a dream more fully you are getting to know your own language, your own images, on what issues your psyche is currently working, and which things matter a lot to you.

Little by little you will find yourself being guided from within, getting help on the problems and facets of your life you've been wondering about. The dream guide does not shame you into being better, or even moralize about your behavior. It simply shows you what you care about, where you might be conflicted, where your feelings are mixed, or some aspects of a relationship you may not have noticed. It will help you find your way through difficult decisions.

How to Work with a Dream:
The Free-Association Method

There are several ways to work on a dream in a journal. Here are some suggestions. In a very short while you will begin to find the best method for you, or mix and match some of these suggestions to find a style of your own.

Always date and title your dream. Use whatever comes to your head, even when you don't know, "Where did that come from?" Sometimes a headline works best or just comes to you, for example, "Man with blue hat finds old dog" or "What was that schoolgirl thinking?" Later, after the dream has "cooled," these titles give clues to what the immediate feeling was.

After you've chosen a dream with which to work, write down your strongest feeling you had in the dream.

Ask yourself, or finish this sentence: This was basically a story about . . . For example, you might answer "This is a story about a boy who encounters trouble at home and runs away" or "A man who is looking for something and can't seem to find it," or "This is the story of a woman who's driving too fast through the fog."

Now begin to make associations to all the people and main images or symbols in the dream. For example, you might write each down and ray off of each in all directions, noting everything that comes to mind when you think of that thing. For example a silver Lexus (car) appears in your dream. What do you think of when you think of that kind of car? You would write down every thought that comes to you, such as: "Expensive, wish I had one, sign of success, Uncle Joe used to have one, I always envied his kids, etc." Let yourself go and write everything down that comes to you, even if you are embarrassed by it. Stay at it a little longer so you get past the first two or three things that come to you. If any of them feel more like the feeling of the dream, mark those or highlight them.

Free-associate to the people in the dream too, write down any memories or feelings you have about them. If the person is a stranger, write down whom they remind you of and where you might meet such a person and how you feel around them.

As you're writing, see what story is starting to emerge from the "hits" or places where something has more feeling, or feels like the dream felt. Try some interpretations to yourself. Write those down. For example, "This dream seems to be telling me that I envy Mark, the guy who just started work and drives that big fancy car, the way I used to envy Uncle Joe. His kids had all the things I wished I could have. Now this guy comes along and seems to be showing me up. I've worked at my company for years, and here comes this hotshot, and its making me mad. I have to talk this over with someone, because it's really starting to upset me!"

As you work with the pieces of the dream, getting associations to the main characters in the dreams and the main images, watch to see what feelings are emerging as a whole story about something in your life right now. Try to find the basic dream story and then ask, "What is this like?" Where am I feeling these kinds of feelings in my life right now? Where am I doing something like this?" For example, a dream about driving too fast in the fog, gives

10

you an immediate sense of having to slow down, be more careful, look around you. The dream is helping you feel how that is, and what you need to do to help yourself stay safe. You might then find the parallel story in your own life by discovering in what area of your life you've been feeling this way—at home, in a relationship, at work, in your career.

This kind of dream work is a way to find how your life is like the dream story. It's a way of cracking the metaphor code, to find how the dream is showing you what your life or some aspect of it is "like" right now, and what might be needed.

Always look for what the dream might be asking you to do to get the help you need, or what you want to do now that you know this.

Chapter Two Points to Remember:
Getting Started with Your Own Dreams

- One of the best ways to learn how to work with a client's dreams is to learn how to listen and respond to your own.
- Keep a pad of paper and pen or small tape recorder by your bed and record everything you remember when you wake. If you can wake without an alarm, lie there and go over the dream for a few minutes before moving around too fast—which tends to break the mood and sometimes loses the dream.
- When you can find some time with a journal, go over the dream free associating to each image.
- Give the dream a title, and see if you can determine on what theme or topic (favorite issue) this dream is focusing.
- What story is this dream telling?
- What is it asking of you or your client?
- Use the template given in chapter two as a framework for working and simply fill in the blanks until you get a feel for working with a dream. See Appendix for worksheets you can copy.

"Dreams contain images and thought associations which we do not create with conscious intent. They arise spontaneously without our assistance and are representatives of a psychic activity withdrawn from our arbitrary will. Therefore the dream is, properly speaking, a highly objective, natural product of the psyche, from which we might expect indications, or at least hints, about certain basic trends in the psychic process."

(C.G. Jung, CW 7, par. 210)

Chapter 3

Using the Free-Association Method with a Client

Using This Technique to Help Someone Else Discover Dream Meanings

A S A THERAPIST, SPIRITUAL DIRECTOR, or life coach you will essentially be using this same technique with your clients, except that you will be guiding them through each part of the dream work. It's important that you have a good grasp of this basic technique using your own dream, so you don't get distracted by the many details in a client's dream and lose the basic dream story. Discovering the basic "spine" of the story is the essence of this method. Only then can you discover how this metaphor is like your own life in some way.

Let's try this method now with an actual dream. Let's say that Marcy, one of the women with whom you have been working for some time, brings in this dream and asks for help understanding it. (Always ask that dreams be written in present tense, and that a copy be given to you so both of you have the text in front of you. Have the client read it aloud. Often the reading out loud triggers further memories and associations.)

Marcy's Dream:
Title: My House Is Standing Open and Flies Are Getting In!

> I am in the back seat of a car, and my mother is driving. As she drives, she's chattering and driving all over the road, not staying to her side, and it's making me nervous. Finally she drives off the main road and up to my house, which looks like it's being remodeled. Huge mounds of dirt are there, as if things are being excavated for a new basement, and the doors are hanging open. I think, oh my, the flies are all getting in!

Ask Marcy what the main feeling of this dream was when she woke. Let's assume she says, "I was shocked that my house is under construction and I didn't even know it!" Or, she might say, "I'm shocked to see that flies are all over my house and I have no doors to hold them out." While in both instances she is expressing the main feeling as shock or surprise, there's a slight shift in emphasis in each of these, isn't there, telling you what the main impact of the dream was for her. In the first she's surprised/shocked that her house is being overhauled, as it were, without her knowledge! In the second, she's shocked and dismayed that flies, irritants, are "bugging her" and she's powerless to keep them out.

Or she might say, "I was so mad at my mother for being so chatty and distracting, and driving so dangerously. I felt like a kid again, in the back seat, with no control at all."

Though each of these aspects of the dream are true, and the dream can carry many layers of feeling and meaning at the same time, you are looking for what was the main feeling or impact of the dream for Marcy. The dream is coming out of her psyche, and her feelings about it are what give you the key to its meaning for her.

You could ask the question another way, by asking, "What is the main story of this dream?" She might say, "This is the story of a person who is reduced to feeling like a child and who finds that even her own house, which she thought was her own adult house, has no control or doors on it."

You can see how this method can take you to the heart of the dream message. However, few people are able to cut through the many details of a dream to its succinct message in this way.

Even if someone does lay out the essence of the story of the dream in a very clear way, it's still important to continue work on the associations to each image. The more layers of feeling and memory the client can add, the more emotional richness is brought to the dream experience. So many accumulated feelings from many years lie behind a single dream. Allowing the complexity of feelings to be talked about is helpful to the dreamer, since gaining clarity about one's own life is one of the goals of therapy.

In the case of the sample dream on which we are working, you would need to ask Marcy what her associations are to these main images: sitting in the back seat of the car, her mother, her mother's chattiness and distractibility (is she really this way in outer life or is this uncharacteristic of her), the car—what kind, does it remind her of any car she has now or in childhood, the mounds of dirt and construction site (does it remind her of any-thing, or any time in her life), her house—what did it look like, does she know any house like it, the doors hanging open, and flies? What do they bring to mind?

As Marcy is responding to the questions you will be asking her in order to understand her associations to each image, note what extra feelings and memories are coming up. You are looking for the connections between the dream presenting this metaphor for her life and her sense of what part of her life could be depicted this way. What aspect of Marcy's life is like this dream? And why did she dream this particular dream now?

Remember always that this dream is Marcy's dream. Even if you think you know what the dream means, if Marcy feels no connection to your interpretation, it is not true for her. It must hit an "Aha point" for the dreamer, some recognition of the truth of the dream for it to be a valid interpretation. In fact it's always best if the dreamer comes up with her own interpretation. If you do venture one of your own, you might say, "If this were my dream, I would think it would mean this. Does that fit?" That way you're acknowledging that you can't entirely know her symbol system, and that the dream came from within her, not you.

It helps if together you venture a guess as to what the dream means, and what the dream might be asking Marcy to do now that she knows this. For example, the dream might be pointing to the fact that Marcy is in a time in her life when she is excavating some old memories and "reconstructing or updating her house." This could mean her work in therapy is effectively beginning to restructure old attitudes and ideas about herself learned from the family system in which she grew up.

Because a house is always renovated for the better, it seems the therapy is having a productive effect. But the doors hanging open and flies coming in could indicate a lack of boundaries. The fact that her mother is driving the car, reminding her of days when as a child she was driven around but was not in control of her destiny, could be showing Marcy that she is still dominated by her mother's attitudes. Her chattiness and distractibility while driving could be a picture of how this contagion spreads to Marcy, causing anxiety. Like a house open to flies, the pesky irritants are getting under Marcy's skin!

The task now would be to talk together about what needs to be done to clear some space for Marcy, create some better boundaries with her mother (and with whomever else she feels un-boundaried) and find some ways to quiet her own chattiness or distractibility if she feels this is also a trait of her own.

Many times a dream figure can point out something about a real character in one's life, in this case Marcy's mother, but also be showing a shadow quality of one's own. The fact that children pick up defenses from parents and then live them out themselves could be talked about. This could be an important teaching moment. As a therapist, you might be able to follow up with some techniques for quieting and calming anxiety—sitting quietly with music or reading, drawing or doodling, or even teaching Marcy simple ways to meditate. In this way she is learning to differentiate herself from her mother. Where her mother distracts herself and even drives others to distraction, Marcy is learning to listen to herself and change the feelings.

You can see how far-reaching work with even one dream can be for gaining insight and changing behavior. You will find therapeutic work with clients deepens when dreams are included along with what each person brings from their life experience from session to session. The inclusion of work with dreams fosters the importance of the inner life—and in the end that is what sustains each person after they have completed their work with you. If a client, patient, directee or counselee takes away a friendship with themselves you have given them a great gift which can never be taken away. You have indeed given them a lasting treasure.

Chapter Three Points to Remember:
Using the Free-Association Method with a Client

- It's easy to get distracted by the many details in a dream. Keep looking for the "spine of the dream," or its main story.
- Ask the client to retell the dream "in a nutshell," looking for the main story.
- Ask the client for the main feeling in the dream, or "What headline would fit this dream?"
- Remember the dream came out of this client, with her whole different-from-your background, experiences, and view of the world. You are safest when you let her try to say what she thinks it means. But you need to guide the work. Help by asking questions and keeping her on track.
- Be aware of how much valuable new information you are getting as you work on dreams about aspects of the client's life he would not think to tell you without this dream "prompt."
- When venturing what you think the dream might mean, you could say something like, "If this were my dream, I might think it meant . . . What do you think? How does that feel?"

"There are a great many 'average dreams' in which a definite structure can be perceived, not unlike that of a drama."

(C.G. Jung, CW 8, par. 561)

Chapter 4

Another Method of Recording and Working with Dreams

ARL JUNG IN HIS VAST WORK on dreams noted that dreams carry the structure of a dramatic work—a play or drama. One of the ways to work with a dream, either your own or a client's, is to use this narrative structure to elucidate the dream. It's a framework that will help you go step by step through the dream to gather information and feelings, with a view to a final interpretation at the end. This technique also incorporates getting personal associations on each symbol from the dreamer, as we did with the Association Method in an earlier chapter, but adds the elements of a play or story to give the dream shape and form. Some therapists like to use this framework almost exclusively, while others try it now and then when they want help organizing a somewhat chaotic or complicated dream. Try it out and see where it might be helpful.

Let's take a look now at how the basic structure of a story or play (or movie) can help us unpack the basic metaphor of a dream.

The Dramatic Structure of a Dream

The basic elements of any novel, story or play are these:

Setting: the story takes place somewhere. This setting is crucial in understanding the basic problem the dream is talking about. In fact, as the authors Whitmont and Pererra put it, the setting is like the "Re:" section of a memo. It alerts you to what the rest of the message or memo will be about. This is also called "exposition" or the "setting of the theme."

For example, in the dream cited in the last chapter, the dream setting is a car, with a mother driving distractedly, and a daughter distressed "in the back seat." This setting is crucial to the dream's message or theme—that the daughter is not in control of her own life, is not driving her own car. In fact, she is being "driven to distraction" by her mother complex. Here the mother complex would be all of the many memories and feelings this daughter has of being mothered in a particular way which still affects her. She still carries the anxieties of her mother, and is trying to re-construct her own house after a different model.

In this dream the setting is a car (one's way of moving around in the world) and from this mother-driven car the daughter sees her own house under construction, being remade or remodeled. This necessary developmental task of adulthood is underway, but it's not finished, and as yet the issues remaining are irritating (flies are bugging her) and boundaries not clear (doors hanging open). The setting helps the rest of the dream make sense.

Always take note of the landscape in which the story is taking place. What place is being depicted? What does this say about the psychological state of the dreamer? Is the setting a serene country side, a busy (or frenetic) freeway, a workplace (how is it the same or different from this person's real work-place)? Is the setting inside a home and, if so, is it one's current home, childhood home, parent's home or a place one has never seen before? What is the condition of this home? (A shabby un-kempt house depicts a different mood from a bright, clean kitchen, for example.) A foreign country, summer camp, motel (temporary), dance studio, prison, or jail all are settings that lit-erally "set us up" to experience the story of the dream differently. Each sets the tone and says, in effect, "from this psychic place in which you are right now, this story follows."

Some dreams are so much about the certain landscape of the dream that the dreamer wakes feeling she "has been some-where." And it's true. She has been transported temporarily out of her own everyday "same old, same old" world, to experience another time and place. Why? What feelings or ideas did this new place elicit? How could your life be different from how it is right now?

Characters: the people or animals or things that are in this story make up the characters.

Who are the people in this dream? Are they people you know? Free-associate off each of them, even if they are strangers. What do you feel around someone like this? Where might you meet such a person? Be sure to note what they are wearing and, like a good director, why they'd be dressed this way. Why was this person used by the dream to tell you something? As casting direc-tor of a play, why would you choose him? To get what point across?

Plot: the activity going on in the story is the plot. In the dream above, mother and daughter are engaged together in some activity or plot. One is driving, the other being driven. Both observe the daughter's house and the state it is in. This is best answered by the question, "What's going on in the dream?"

Crisis or Climax: What is the point of greatest feeling or intensity in the story?

The dreamer can tell you where she was most frightened, or was shocked or angry or most moved by grief or love.

Resolution or ending: (called "Lysis" in Greek drama) How does the conflict resolve itself, or doesn't it? This gives you some idea as a therapist whether the psyche has yet come up with a solution, or is still casting around for one. In the car/house dream, the dream ego is shocked at the end of the dream, and the dream ends there. What she does about her shock will take her to a new place, and further dreams can suggest what that new place feels like to her then.

Chapter Four Points to Remember:
Another Method of Working with Dreams

- Besides the free-associating to every image way of working with a dream, there is another method Carl Jung especially liked, working with the structure of a dream as drama.
- Each element of a drama or movie is pulled out and looked at separately, until the sense of the dream starts to appear.
- Setting, characters, plot, climax of the plot, resolution (or lack of one) are written in as you work with a client, or alone in a journal. You can ask your client to come with some of this pre-work done before a session.
- You are still looking for what is the main story of this dream. What is it asking of me or the client?
- Another way of asking this is, "What do I need in my life that I'm not currently allowing myself?
- Another good question is "Why did I (or to your client), why did you dream this dream now?" ("Why did you need this dream now?")
- See Appendix for work sheets you can copy.

"*The psyche is a self-regulating system that maintains its equilibrium just as the body does. Every process that goes too far immediately and inevitably calls forth compensations . . . whereby those thoughts, inclinations, and tendencies which in conscious life are too little valued come spontaneously into action during the sleeping state.*"

(C.G. Jung, CW 16, par. 330;
CW 8 par. 466)

Chapter 5

How Dreams Facilitate Change

N THIS MANUAL WE ARE RELYING on a basically Jungian style of working with dreams. This means that, where Freud believed that each dream was sexual in content (all symbols were assumed to be symbols of sexuality) and all some form of wish fulfillment, Jung believes that dreams are serving many different functions. He believed that the dream is a "just so" metaphor for some aspect of the dreamer's life.

So a dream might be telling a story of a conflict you are currently living but haven't seen in just this way. It may add elements that cast the dream ego as hero or victim, as uninvolved in its own struggle, an observer maybe, or depict the dreamer as a young boy or girl in the childhood home. That would certainly explain why the conflict is so painful—the dream showing how this present conflict is a replay of some previous struggle as a child in the family setting.

At any rate, the dream is making use of a language we hardly know, using symbols that are the exact meaning the unconscious is trying to express. Much of dream work is learning our own language. Let's face it, many of us are living in bodies we hardly know, and sometimes we learn about only through exhaustion or illness. Likewise our psyches are little known to us. Sometimes we experience them only as an outbreak of feeling that surprises and bewilders us with its sudden power. "I don't know what got into me," we say later, trying to explain, "I never yell and suddenly there I had gone ballistic!"

This very experience of the mysteriousness and different-ness of our inner world and how it sometimes breaks in on us, is what Jung called the experience or possession by a "feeling toned complex." He believed that a complex started with some inner wounding or psychic "bruise," or some positive attraction that we forever remember at a deeper level, a "positive complex," and that further experiences or events, similar memories or inner fantasies cluster around this core feeling, acting like a magnet. This magnetic attraction pulls people toward us that fit this complex of energies, all sides of it, and help create the patterns we habitually live over and over. It's as if we "can't get off the train."

In our waking life, we know little about how our inner world is experiencing this conflict or experience. Let's say you've just taken a job you think you're glad you got, yet you find yourself having a hard time getting there every day, and are constantly late. You've called in sick already three times in the first five weeks. On the surface you're "glad to be working," but seem unaware that you don't like the job, or how you feel when you're there, or the boss, and are finding ways to sabotage it!

A dream could help you sort this out, help you face the conflict and decide what to do about it, rather than letting events run their course, and you losing the job, and getting a bad job history.

So a dream contains "news" from the world within us. Much of the pain in our lives is about the separation and alienation we feel from outer world to our inner world. We put a face on things for our husbands and wives, friends, and coworkers, but the person we are really fooling is ourselves. Working back and forth from outer world experience of everyday life to inner world, and all the things it wants to say and feel but is restricted from expressing, is an integrative work of the highest importance.

Psychoanalyst Carl Jung's view of the psyche is that it is purposive and helpful, an inner guide which comments on everything which we care about and are living in our everyday lives. He did not believe that every longing or concern was linked to sexual or aggressive instinct, as Freud believed. He did not believe that each of us was burdened with the Oedipal or Electra complex, begun in infancy, when boys desired their mothers and felt their fathers to be rivals, or girls desired their fathers and felt their mother's disapproval for it.

Though there are people and family dynamics where this is a real and marked conflict, perhaps buried in memory, Jung did not believe this was everyone's core complex. And he did not believe like Alfred Adler, who also did some early work with Freud and then left him to found his own school of psychology, that everyone had a core inferiority or superiority complex.

In fact, Jung saw that every normal person had a set of complexes which made up his unique psychic structure. He saw that these were the important issues the person cared about or which preoccupied that person. Over and over through the years, these same issues would show themselves—in relationships, or concerns, conflicts, loves, passions, or struggles. He respected these complexes as the building blocks of the psyche, and saw that each person needed to be aware of these and acknowledge how they affected his/her life.

Dreams are a wonderful way to see how these complexes live us along. As we get conscious of them they tend not to blindside us or surprise us so much with their power. Basically, every person who walks into your office for therapy is expressing a need to find a troubling complex and begin to understand it. For one it is a persistent need to control or be the center of things. Over and over she might turn people off, but can't see the problem, can't understand why, as she puts it, "people are so controlling." (People often project their main complex onto other people and blame them for their unhappiness.)

Or another feels like he always gets the short end of any situation. Someone else always gets the bonus or pay raises rightfully his. He finds this happening at work, on vacations ("someone else got the beachside room, ours looked onto the parking lot"), and now his marriage is threatened. ("Sure, I'll be the only one in my family to get a divorce. What is wrong with me?")

Most often, though you as therapist or counselor can see the sabotaging thought pattern, the person living it cannot. So the dream, as Jung understood it, can helpfully show us the stories in which these conflicts or complexes enter our lives. Sometimes a dream will show the origin of a complex, how it got started in another time and place. Sometimes it shows another person or character noted for this same behavior in a client's dream, and the client slowly begins to see where this could be a "shadow figure," with some likenesses to himself. Slowly this client could begin to "withdraw the projection," note that the problem is not all out there, but within himself and the way he's learned to think and protect himself.

This is an enormous moment in therapy, or spiritual direction or counseling of any kind. The client is enlarging his own notion of himself to include some not-so-nice parts he's always thought were "someone else's fault." But accepting this shadow means he's also finding where these thought patterns keep him in a rut, program him for the same set of problems over and over, keep him a prisoner of a default mode he may have outgrown long ago. Now he is ready to find other ways of thinking and relating that are not tied up in this complex. Dreams can be a source of help in this new place, too.

Because dreams do not work from a base of shame or moralizing, they seem like a compassionate friend, guiding this person to view himself as simply human, not the bad person he was taught to avoid. Self acceptance is the beginning of a new attitude. You as therapist, and the dream world as guide, can help a client modify what has been a crippling complex or persistent self-defeating pattern, to find a better way.

Chapter Five Points to Remember:
How Dreams Facilitate Change

- Our ego ideal, or who we think we are, is only a small piece of the whole of who we are. Much of ourselves is hidden, even to ourselves.
- We are often surprised by an uprush of feeling which we explain later as "I was totally beside myself! I don't know what got into me." It's a part of ourselves we hardly recognize.
- These are "complexes" or centers of feeling around certain topics or issues. Jung called the nucleus of a complex its "archetypal core" because each is universally known. An example of such a universal theme would be "the abandoned child," or "the jealous spouse." People over all generations or cultures seem to know these feelings. Each of us has an especially strong set of past experiences which make us vulnerable to being triggered into the complex again. Often we're not aware of them until something comes into our life that activates these strong feelings. Then we can say that a complex is "constellated."
- Though Freud believed we all have the same core complex, the Oedipal Complex, which was basically sexual in nature and aggressive in tone, Carl Jung saw that we each have our own unique set of complexes caused by past experiences, and that it is normal to have them. They organize our psyches.
- It is, however, up to us to sort out our complexes and get to know them so we're not blindsided or crippled by them, or caught in habitual patterns of hurting other people with them.
- This is why your clients are working with you: to get some insight into how their own psyches work, what complexes are hot-button issues for them, and to learn ways to recognize and stop repeating destructive patterns.
- Dreams can begin to help people get to know themselves, what matters to them, what their patterns are, where their strengths can help them out.

- In fact, dreams help people befriend themselves. As a therapist or guide, you've given them a great gift if they leave therapy having learned to like, trust, and respect themselves.

"If we want to interpret a dream correctly, we need a thorough knowledge of the conscious situation at the moment, because the dream contains its unconscious complement, that is, the material which the conscious situation has constellated in the unconscious. Without this knowledge it it impossible to interpret a dream correctly, except by a lucky fluke."

(C.G. Jung, CW 8, par. 477)

Chapter 6

Some Common Dream Themes

S YOU WORK WITH DREAMS, your own as well as your clients', you will notice that there are some common themes that tend to show up at key times or phases in a dreamer's life. Carl Jung saw these as archetypal patterns built into human nature. For example all humans, no matter where they live, experience developmental stages: birth, early infancy, childhood, adolescence, young adulthood, middle age, old age, preparing for and facing death. Likewise, we all share some common dilemmas and challenges in negotiating these stages of life. We have common hopes and fears, bridges which must be crossed in moving from one stage of life to another, from a young me-centered life to relating to others through different phases of maturity.

Because these large concerns are common to us all, our dreams move through and focus on the themes that we are currently working on. Finding the theme in a dream or issue the dream is related to can help situate the client or dreamer in his/her current life phase and current life task. That can then shed light on the unique dream plot used by this dream to elucidate this particular theme.

Some Universal Themes

Crossing a street at an intersection or "four-way stop," crossing a bridge or a river, crossing from one place to another. This is a dream you might expect when someone is indeed at a crossroads. During crucial "intersections" in the dreamer's life, the dream landscape will reflect the intersection of various possible paths, or the feeling of "things coming at me from all directions." Crossing over from one place to another, or being at the start of that journey in the dream, will signal to you that this person is indeed ready for a new direction, or ready to proceed further on the path they have chosen. Often discussing this image and theme with its possible meanings for this person at this time will yield the accompanying fears and anticipations, as well as the blocks that might be holding the dreamer back. Look for obstructions or clear paths to note what the psychic landscape reveals about these fears or hopes and what is needed to proceed.

Dreams of falling. Note where the person is falling from. What situation causes the sensation or anxiety of falling to set in? This gives you some idea of the theme being activated here. Is it fear of "failing"/falling and in what area (academic, job performance, relationship, marriage, parenting, career goals)? Some falling dreams, especially when a person is learning something new, or trying to incorporate a new attitude (learning to trust, for example, where a person has previously been cynical or sarcastic), can show the ego trying to hold on to the old way and fearing what it expects to be a harsh fall. The "fall into a new way" may be a step into growth, but the dream shows how afraid the whole defense system is of such a new move. As a therapist, this is your chance to discern with your client what the new way would be, what fears surround this new move, and why. Then together you can build some support systems needed for the new attitude or life change.

Dreams of failing or not being prepared for an exam, an important meeting or challenge at work or school. First, as in all work with dreams, look at the literal meaning. Is there some task the dreamer admits to avoiding? Is the dream a simple help to get back on task and complete something he will regret if he doesn't? If the dreamer doesn't relate at this literal level, explore any area of life that is making requests for attention but being ignored. How does the dreamer feel he or she is being "put to the test," not ready for a challenge?

Who or what (internal or external) is judging them and finding them inadequate? Could this be a transference dream in which you, their therapist, are seen as judge who sees them as not measuring up to the task? Look for clues in the dream for answers to these questions, and for emotional resonance with the dreamer.

Dreams of being chased, intruded on, robbed, victimized, frightened by a "foreign figure." Is the figure identifiable, familiar, a stranger? Describe the character—ever seen anyone like this in life, movies, video? "He was kind of like . . ." is a good way to start, and, "Where might you see a guy like this?" is a good follow-up question. You, as therapist, are looking for the qualities this dreamer associates with the intruding figure. These, if it is same sex as the dreamer, may be "shadow qualities" the dreamer has shut out of his own personality and now come back angry and push the dreamer to an extreme. The idea is that what we denounce as "not I" shows up with the same attitude the ego is using to denounce it. Only with some effort to see where this quality might also live in the dreamer does one reach a more relational tone, a not-so-one-sided judgmental attitude. It does not mean the dreamer has to like this figure or be like him, but some acknowledgement that she too could be driven to do this helps balance out a too-rigid attitude, "I hate him. I would never do that."

Looking at life situations is also crucial here, to see if the dream is in some way signaling a warning—some danger seen or sensed peripherally and not sufficiently heeded. This is the literal level and, as with every dream, should be looked at first before proceeding to the metaphorical level.

Dreams of losing things—wallet, purse, sums of money, ID cards. Is there any real thing lost or almost lost (or retrieved) recently? Does the dreamer have too casual an attitude toward something she says she values but treats too cavalierly?

How does the dreamer feel she might be losing what she cares about? How is her identity (ID card) jeopardized? Is she getting credit (lost credit cards) for what she is doing at work or in her family? In other words, how is this dream true? Why was this dream story told to this dreamer NOW?

Dreams of wearing strange or inappropriate or uncharacteristic clothes—or being naked. Generally, clothes in a dream are about the ability to wear the right clothes for the occasion, i.e., to fit socially. Clothes are the adaptive persona or way we make ourselves fit or work in different roles. If a dream showed someone wearing "plastic" clothes, for example, or a tux where everyone else is in a relaxed mode, in jeans and flannel shirts, the question would be what keeps you from relaxing? Why do you have to be formal, rigid, and stiff? How might this be a recurring theme in this person's life—trying to measure up, be good enough, and have enough of what it takes for the role.

Nudity on the other hand could be exactly about this inability to have enough social grace, enough "social cover," or feeling "exposed" in certain situations. The rest of the dream clues and "textual context" can help determine where this inadequacy is felt —in what settings this feeling is particularly acute.

Dreams of flying. How is this person feeling "high," really super good, or ungrounded or "inflated" or out of touch with their humanity? Where might the dreamer be trying to escape, "get above it all," and why? Is the dream compensatory—for example, where persons have too low an opinion of themselves, too "low to the ground," the dream might compensate by showing them their "flying high" visionary abilities. Exploring the rest of the dream context and discussing "how flying felt" will help both of you determine which of these is being depicted in the dream. Again, why did this dream come now?

Dreams of houses. Moving into a new house, remodeling an old one, finding new rooms in a house, exploring attic or basement, being back in a childhood home. If the house is indicative of the self, or the place within oneself where one lives, then a "new house" would represent a new shift, new growth, and a new place from which to stand and live. New rooms would be new aspects of oneself that are now "coming open," revealing a certain readiness for change, or good moves already made in that direction, and would certainly signal a successful turn in the therapy. Exploring what these changes are and how that feels true, how one is feeling more expansive, would be good directions to take in exploring the implications of such a dream.

Remodeling dreams, even if construction is messy, would indicate that with time something new in which to live will be available. Some new attitude which feels difficult now is being seen by the psyche as a good permanent value, being "built on" to the current structure. Transformation is being worked at, and a new house or remodeled house is actively under construction.

Being in one's childhood home may indicate looking at a current issue through the eyes of an attitude learned at home, which may or may not be adequate to one's adult life. "How did it feel to be at home as a child?" is a good question to ask. "How old were you in this dream?" "What happened to you at that age?" and, "Who else was in this dream?" are good follow-up questions. Is there any way in which the dreamer feels like he is in his childhood place in his current life? Are there any people who currently remind him of old family patterns?

Dreams of death, yourself or someone you know (or a stranger) dying. As with any dream, check this out in outer reality. Is the person fearing a parent's death and, as it were, rehearsing how they will cope? Has someone recently died? What comes immediately to mind from the dream, and what feelings well up? Sometimes the experience of the dream brings up feelings left over from a previous grief which are asking to be recognized and processed.

Many death dreams, however, are symbolic and are related to something in the dreamer's life which is dying off. Dreams of a parent long dead, for example, may be about a quality, attitude, or "force field" that person exuded and is starting to wane. Sometimes a person is so driven to repeat a parent's story that he can't get to his own. A son with a father who failed in business and who now can't seem to get off the ground to have what he wants in life or career goals, might dream of his father's death when he takes the first step towards breaking "that family jinx."

Always explore both literal real deaths in the dreamer's life and, if that has no immediate emotional valence, check out which areas of one's life are changing. Where is there a death of something and what new thing is growing in its place? Remember, pre-cognitive dreams, which prefigure or foretell someone's death are extremely rare. Occasionally you will run into someone with a history of having them, or an ancestral trait runs in the family. "I have what they tell me my great-grandmother had—she predicted my uncle's death." Most times the dreamer is being told about herself and what feels dead now to her, or what hold over her is dying off.

Dreaming of someone who has died gives one a chance to continue the relationship, finish off what might still be festering or feels undone, say what one wishes she could have said, or complete his experience of the departed who is still emotionally present.

Dreams of babies, small children. Look carefully at what the emotion is as well as the condition of the children in the dream. Is the child lost, crying, neglected, starved, happy, contented, and playing? These are usually messages about one's own inner child. Checking on the condition and age of the child may help the dreamer tune in to lost or neglected dreams, or find what has happened that number of years ago and where that dream or emotional tone is now. If a dream says one hasn't fed a baby for a long time, it might be a signal to tune into whatever that baby or new beginning was, and brings it into a more central "nourished" part of one's life. Dreams of being pregnant or giving birth are often about something new growing within, or the birth of something new in one's life.

These are just some of the themes common to many dreamers. However, for each dreamer the story and setting is tailor-made and has a unique meaning to that dreamer which must be explored. Don't let the dreamer settle for an easy answer: "I had this dream because I'm in midlife." The more specific the dreamer can be, the more clarity he/she gains.

Chapter Six Points to Remember:
Some Common Dream Themes

- Dream dictionaries are not helpful because they homogenize dream images into one size fits all, quick merchandizing. One such dream dictionary claimed, "If you dream of eating a meal, it means you need to look at your business deals." Each dream comes out of a person's own life and experiences. Trust your own good sense. Meals are about food, nourishment, good company or about your own experience of food, family, and what these bring to mind.
- However, there are some common themes that many people dream about. Feel out the sense of an image—and explore from there. Try a symbol book for symbol meanings over various times and cultures.
- For example, dreams of being at an intersection tend to be just that. Someone is at the crossroads. Explore the personal meanings in this. Why? What's going on?
- Likewise dreams of falling, taking exams, being chased, or being lost all lend themselves to exploring what right now in your life is LIKE this.
- Feeling out the dream together with your client is a good way into the sense of the image. For example, asking, "How does it feel to be the only person at a party with the wrong clothes or with bare feet?" can help sort out where in her present life your client is feeling inadequate.

"*The psychological context of dream-contents consists in the web of associations in which the dream is naturally embedded. It should, therefore, be an absolute rule to assume that every dream, and every part of a dream, is unknown at the outset, and to attempt an interpretation only after carefully taking up the context. We can then apply the meaning we have thus discovered to the text of the dream itself and see whether this yields a fluent reading or, rather, a satisfying meaning emerges.*"

(C.G. Jung, CW 12, par. 48)

Chapter 7

Dreams as Helps in the Clinical Process

 REAMS ARE A CONSTANT SOURCE of guidance to the thera-
pist, life coach, spiritual director, and counselor. In his book
Dreams and Healing, Jungian analyst John Sanford wrote:

"Suppose someone told you that there was something that
spoke to you every night, that always presented you with a
truth about your own life and soul, that was tailor-made to
your individual needs and particular life story, and that offered
to guide you throughout your lifetime and connect you with
a source of wisdom far beyond yourself. And, furthermore,
suppose all of this was absolutely free. Naturally, you would
be astonished that something like this existed. Yet this is exactly the way it is with dreams."

This is true for the individual, but it's doubly true for the person attempting to work with or companion another. As therapist,
your dreams can be sources of knowledge and insight into the client,
who also has dreams and guidance from within him-/herself, too.
These dreams are a constant source of help regarding what is best
for this client, indeed what is being asked for from within this person.

It is also, as an added bonus, a source of help for you the therapist, a kind of gentle inner supervisor, regarding transference and countertransference feelings, intuitions, observations.

The Dream's Help with Assessment

Let's look first at the client and how his or her dreams can help with your first sessions in which you are hearing his story, assessing what will be needed, devising a therapeutic plan, and a diagnosis/prognosis. In Jungian theory, the "initial dream" is seen as one of the first dreams a client brings to you to be looked at together. This is always a comment at some level on the issue of trust, since looking at the way the dream is presented to you indicates the client's putting trust in your abilities to see into his story, to know more than has previously been available to him, to join him in discovering inner sources of wisdom.

The "initial dream" has the capacity to give an overview of what this person's psychic landscape is at this time, what work might be called for in your sessions together. The dream can tell you what particular complexes or issues this person is dealing with right now. And the dream can give you a glimpse into the overall emotional climate in which this person is now living, by letting you experience for yourself the tone of the dream—desperation, hope, cynicism, stress and strain, or excitement over the potential for help.

Dream Helps with Transference/Countertransference Issues

This first dream can also tell you whether the person has habitual attitudes of which he/she may be unaware but which will affect your work together. If a parental or authority complex is getting in the way, it will definitely affect you in your attempt to create a good working alliance with this patient. Even a positive transference to you needs to be viewed for what it is—a transferring of feelings from another time and place onto you. For better or for worse, you are being viewed through a screen or color not of your own making. It is important to be aware of this.

The dream can help you out here. Look carefully at the dream to see how you might be depicted, in disguise, in the dream? Is there any figure that could be taken as a symbol of a caregiver or helper, authority, or parent? How is the dream ego (client) dealing with or feeling about this figure? This will tell you something of what this client's habitual attitude tends to be toward the authority or help you represent. Since he hardly knows you, this being one of your first meetings, you can assume much of what is being felt in the dream is being "transferred" from another time and place to you, who are standing in the place of some past helper, or authority (or parent) at this time.

Let's look at some examples of initial dreams and what kind of information each can yield. First, here is a dream which shows the dreamer's psychic situation or emotional climate in which she lives:

A forty-five-year-old woman dreams:
"I am standing in the garden looking at all the dead plants. How did this happen, I wonder out loud. It's too early for frost. Just then a neighbor's child comes darting through, trampling some of the flowers that are blooming. "Hey!" I yell. "Stop that, you little hellion!" But she just turns around and grins and runs on. It makes me mad, but there's nothing I can do about it."

You would use what you know about helping a dreamer free-associate to the images in the dream to get to the basic story and its connection to her present life. But what would you know from the dream about the dreamer's present dilemma, and "the story under the story," for which she is seeking your help?

What are these dead "plants?" Are they in any way dead "plans"? Could they be something hoped for in early life that died along the way? What is meant by the child overrunning the garden? Is there any young aspect of herself to which she feels out of touch or unrelated? Maybe an aspect that habitually gets away from her conscious control and causes her to say or do things she later regrets? Does she have energy at her disposal, or does her everyday life feel like dead plants—with child energy cut off and running wild, working against her, not for her.

It is helpful to look for polarities or opposites in dreams as possibly being two ends of a spectrum. In this dream, dead plants are at one end, child energy at the other. She is standing in the middle feeling she has no control over either. From where in her life story is this hopelessness or dejection coming? How does disconnection with her own children or inner children create a dead garden? What seems to be needed to regain happiness?

By talking these things over with her, you would have access to so much more information, feelings, and history than this woman might have thought to tell you on her own. Let's face it, since most people come in with a specific presenting problem, they are often unaware of how far-reaching and helpful therapy, or any form of companioning, direction, or coaching, can be for their whole lives. So they tend to select out what aspects they think you need, to problem-solve this one issue, unaware of how habitual attitudes and patterns color and shape their lives.

Next let's look at how an initial dream can help you with not only a sense of what this person needs at this point in his life, but also what habitual attitudes might underlie the problem, and become a transference issue in your work together. Many therapists will find that what they were taught about transference or countertransference in their study of psychology was inadequate or outdated. Contrary to some older writings, transference is not something only psychoanalysts encounter, or worse "foster." It is simply a fact of life whenever two people meet and talk. Projection of what this person is for me, even in a simple conversation, is always present, known or not.

Because projection is a constant ingredient of your work with others, it is of utmost importance that you stay aware of and conscious of it working in the room with you. You are being seen by the client as yourself and more than yourself. You may be cast in the role of beloved father or teacher, or as "another one of those inept men who can't see beyond their own needs." As a woman, you may be seen on the surface by some as a helper, maternal figure, or a seductress. Colored by a client's past issues with her mother or sisters, you may even be seen as an interfering meddler. Even tone of voice can set such a person off. Suddenly you find distrust, or sharpness in the client's retort after what you meant to be helpful advice, and you know you are getting a transference reaction.

What is important is that this is a piece of emotional information that you have stumbled onto. You would need at this point to watch your own countertransference reaction here. If you are tempted to retaliate, you know she has touched a nerve! There are many insightful writings on this topic, most of them written by psychoanalysts, Freudian or Jungian. Analysts have always specialized in observing and working at this depth level (mindful of how the unconscious affects everyday interactions) especially within the therapeutic encounter.

Here is a dream which signals to you, the therapist, that there will be strong transference issues at work in your ensuing therapy.

A fifty-year-old man dreams:

"I enter a shop, like a carpenter shop, and walk around looking at the tools. There's a man there who seems to be suspicious, as if he's thinking I'm going to steal something. I walk toward the door, but then turn and say some pleasantries to him so he'll think better of me. He turns away and pretends he's busy. He picks up an old slouch hat from the corner and puts it on. Now he looks like my dad who never thought I would amount to anything! I feel kind of sick and slink out the back door."

What transference issues can you expect to be revisiting within this therapy? And what attitudes are indeed "making your client sick" as he faces his life? Helping the client see how this attitude wearies him and makes him his own enemy will be needed in this work. And if you are a male therapist, you will need to side-step his mistrust and assumption that you too, like his father, will be not only suspicious of his good intentions, but secretly sure that he will not ever amount to anything.

The dream can be an extremely helpful guide in monitoring this, his core complex. This first dream will stand as a baseline dream, from which variations on the theme can be read over time. The dream is giving guidance to the dreamer, as if saying, "Whatever else you tell this therapist about your problems, don't forget to tell him about your lifelong struggle with your dad."

And the dream is helping you, the therapist, by saying in effect, "Some of what you experience with this client will be old attitudes that predate you. So don't get too bent out of shape or caught in his unconscious messages. Stay steady and help him see where he's setting you up to say things his dad would have said. He needs to find out that he carries his dad around with him as an internal attitude toward himself, and expects people, even 'recruits' people, to act that way towards him now."

You can see what an additional monitoring help to the therapist dreams can be. And, dreams do have a tendency to "cut to the chase" and give you information the client would not think to tell you in the first several sessions.

Dreams Help with Diagnosis/Prognosis

Let's look now at the issue of diagnosis/prognosis and how an early dream can help. Since treatment plans are built off of diagnosis, it's clear how important initial assessment is in the work ahead. But helpful also is your sense of this person as someone suffering his or her own humanity—"the slings and arrows" of being a certain typology, or of being an introvert or extrovert in a setting which calls for the opposite, or of having formed habitual patterns of defense in response to difficulties or even abuse or trauma in early or later life.

Sometimes someone presents with a clear case of living a parent's complexes, but more often all of this is hidden under the story this client selects to say. Out of all she could have said, this is the story or piece of it that you are being told. And this story is what you have to go on. When people bring dreams into the therapy, they are bringing you "the rest of the story."

A client who might present as a person in deep clinical depression, may, through the dream story, reveal more hope than she is currently aware of. For example, one extremely depressed woman dreamed of parking a black trailer home near a creek where she woke to find masses of wildflowers. This dream would be giving clues as to prognosis, i.e., that her psyche seems to be prepared to give over to other, more positive feelings if given some help.

In terms of diagnosis, an initial dream could reveal potential psychosis, which would be an indication not to proceed with dream work, or other work where the unconscious could potentially overpower the weak ego. Instead, strengthening a person's ties with his conscious life would be called for. Learning how to become more skillful in relating to people or work life, learning basics of living "in the world" with some comfort and lessening distress, might be of ultimate importance.

Most experienced therapists would already have a kind of sixth sense that this person is "treading close to the edge" and has a precarious hold on reality. A dream then would simply confirm one's belief and help in that way with diagnosis. Such dreams might be those where the surroundings are devoid of people, or civilization, or where the person representing the dreamer (the "dream ego") is utterly overwhelmed with chaotic elements, mutilations, completely walled in or unable to cope.

"Chaotic, irrational jumps in the dream imagery, for example, may suggest borderline pathology," warn Whitmont and Perera, two Jungian analyst authors of an excellent book, *Dreams a Portal to the Source*. In their book, Chapter 10, "Prognosis in Dreams," is invaluable for more information on discerning pathology through the initial or follow-up dreams. They are quick to advise not using dreams as part of therapy with such an unstable person, or at such an unstable time in this person's life.

If a person has a strong fear of dreams, or shows resistance to this kind of inner exploration, it's wise not to override their defenses. They may reveal in further work what aspects of their life they fear opening up. Better to stay with their day-to-day lives and give them the support for their present needs than to push them past their own good instincts for protection.

Likewise, do not push a client to see "what you are sure the dream means and they need to see." A dream is always more effective when you can arrive at its meaning together. If a person has active resistance to seeing some aspects of the dream's meanings, he may need some time to find his way to them. There is always the chance, as well, that your meanings are simply not their meanings. Or it may be that this person cannot accept meaning translated by another until she can find her own words for it. This kind of struggle, however, a therapist wanting to teach or push a meaning or worse, moralize a client and his/her struggle not to accept it, would be worth looking at together to see where it may be a reenactment from the past. It is always a good thing to get supervision at such a juncture as well. Never simply push past a client's defenses. Something important is always being expressed in this "disturbance in the field" which needs to be understood and "seen into." Often this can lead to a breakthrough and deeper healing through your effort to really hear what is being expressed through his/her reluctance.

In summary, dreams can provide you with clues to this person's ability to do depth work, or their readiness to grow and change. An initial dream can warn you that the unconscious threatens to overwhelm this very weak ego, which might already be having trouble discerning outer from inner reality. Anyone with a pathology that tends to confuse the two (delusional at any level) should not be encouraged to work with dreams.

Chapter Seven Points to Remember:
Dreams as Helps in the Clinical Process

- Initial dreams and transference countertransference dreams give valuable information you, as a clinician, need to process and assess.
- Do not push past a client's resistance if she/he does not want to bring you dreams. Honor these as still necessary defenses.
- If a client is having trouble discerning fantasy from reality, or has a weak ego structure that keeps him unable to cope with ordinary everyday events, do not complicate things by working with dreams. Build ego functioning instead.
- Many people are both drawn to dreamwork in therapy, but also somewhat afraid of dreams as "giving them away," or worried you'll see too much of them and see "I'm really sicker than I thought." Help them with a good book, suggest a dream workshop if one is available, or an article you've read and trust.
- It can be helpful to work with a dream analyst when you feel you're stuck or can't discern what's going on in your own or a client's dreams.

"It is plain foolishness to believe in ready-made systematic guides to dream interpretation, as if one could simply buy a reference book and look up a particular symbol. No dream symbol can be separated from the individual who dreams it . . . each individual varies so much in the way his unconscious complements or compensates his conscious mind that it is impossible to be sure how far dreams and their symbols can be classified at all."

(C.G. Jung, *Man and His Symbols*, pp. 38, 42)

Chapter 8

Different Functions of Dreams

OMETIMES A DREAM SEEMS confusing until the question is asked, What is this dream trying to do for the dreamer? There are a number of ways dreams function, and knowing them can be helpful, especially when you can't find another way into the dream.

As you've probably learned by now in your own reading and dream work, all dreams are not created equal. Some dreams, for example, seem like each figure or object in the dream is a part of the dreamer, or represents a feeling this dreamer has about a certain issue. In this case, asking him to relate to each, or "become" each image, yields multifaceted insight. For example, a man dreams about a "chaotic day" where the engine of his car burns out and can't be driven anymore, and an angry bystander tells him to "move this crate out of my backyard!" Since cars often represent the body, or the way we move through life and "get around," could this dream be a somatic (body) dream? The dream could be telling a man who "is on overdrive" that he is burning himself out.

In this case, you might use the Gestalt method popularized by Fritz Perls, of becoming or speaking as each part of the dream. You could ask the dreamer to tell how it feels to be a "burned out engine who can't take it anymore" or "isn't going to be 'driven' anymore." Then, you might ask this same dreamer to speak as the driver, then as the man whose backyard is intruded on by this car, and finally as the "old abandoned crate" itself. This welter of feelings, all contained in the dream under different images, may be the dream's effort to wake this person up to a whole set of related feelings pressing in on him.

You can see how much emotional information is being given here: the conflicted feelings of overwork, fear of being abandoned as useless or "put out to pasture," fear of other people's criticism. This is "felt" or experienced information, probably much more than this man would have gained access to if you had simply asked, "How is your work life going."

However, all dreams do not lend themselves to this method. Part of gaining experience in working with dreams is getting a feel for which dreams do work well with the Gestalt method, and which are too complicated or still too far from a patient's consciousness for him to identify with. Generally speaking, dreams that work well for working with each part of the dream as part of oneself are those in which the patient recognizes many of the feelings in the dream as her own. In other words, the function of some dreams seems to be to dramatize the many feelings that go with an issue or event. The fact that all these conflicted feelings are going on at the same time causes anxiety. Sorting them out through this kind of dream work can bring a sense of clarity and relief.

What are some other ways dreams can work? Some dreams are simply a statement of how things are right now. Jung called this function a "just so" statement of present reality. This kind of dream is reflecting how one feels right now—not a day or a week from now, but right now. It's important to reflect this back to the client, that the dream is not predicting, not saying this condition will remain this way, but stating, "This is how things appear to you. This is how you feel they are right now."

Sometimes people are surprised to know they feel this way. They might have foreclosed on some situation, written somebody off, and not even known they have. Remember, there is always news in a dream of some kind. Look carefully at the dream to see what has been brought from the unconscious (or unknown) to consciousness. Sometimes it's the setting—a bizarre setting for a routine, or already known action in the dream, could mean the dreamer has never looked at this situation "in this light," or "from this place."

Other dreams function as a metaphor for what is currently going on. Expressions such as "I feel like I'm running on empty," "walking uphill against a wind," "sliding down a slippery slope," "driving with one foot on the gas, one on the brake," "walking alone at night in a strange city," "can't find my way home," are all metaphorical statements in common use. Any one of them could be a dream. Finding the parallel ("What is this like?") in real life, is the way to work with a metaphor dream. What do you wish? Or what do you need? Or need to do? is a helpful follow-up to such a dream.

Some dreams are working in a compensatory way to reality. Where a person's conscious attitude is too one-sided, a dream may come to compensate by depicting the opposite attitude. For example, a client may be fixated on her shyness and inability to talk to people she doesn't know. The dream may show her in a setting where she is comfortable, and reveal how she forgets herself when she's teaching or showing someone how to do a hobby she loves.

Or conversely, if someone brags about being accepting of everyone, but has a dream revealing her snide and "catty" side, the dream is again compensating a part of the truth with that which is also true. Part of maturity is being able to accept the truth of one-self, shadow and all, which leads to acceptance of others and their shadow parts, too. So these dreams bring the dreamer "the rest of the story" without judgment or shame. The dream guide seems to be a friend interested in wholeness rather than perfection.

A dream may also be complimentary to the conscious atti-tude. Sometimes a dream affirms a decision one has just made or adds to the new insight one has just gotten. The dream agrees, say-ing, in effect, "Yes, that is true." For example, after struggling with years of overwork, or addiction, a man dreams of himself in a serene setting just after making a call to schedule a retreat. The dream seems to be affirming or complimentary (rather than com-pensatory) to what he has decided he needs. Sometimes such a dream can support the dreamer when he is trying new behavior you have talked with him about in a session, but for which he gets little support in his current life setting. This kind of inner approval can help him stay with the new behavior when all his old familiar patterns want to kick in.

Still other dreams seem to show "the anatomy of a com-plex." They show us what the basic story of a particular complex is and who the essential players are in it. For example, after a big fight with her husband over his gambling habit, a woman dreams of being five years old in her old childhood home. She sees that her mother is worried, her father is drinking, the house is filled with tension and fear of "an explosion on the way." She starts to set the table, do the dishes, in a panicked attempt to change the mood. When she wakes she feels "unbearably anxious, out of con-trol, powerless."

Here the dream shows what story gets reenacted, along with all the feelings from her five-year-old life, whenever addictive behavior triggers the fear that "he will not take care of me. I know he cares more about his addiction than he does me, and I'm on my own." The dream shows this woman the origin of her complex, the age she was at the time, and what developmental tasks may have been injured during this time. It seems her autonomy is wounded, she keeps finding men "just like my current husband." The dream also shows what defenses habitually kick in to try to protect her. "I get excessively busy" (the five-year-old in the dream, full of anxiety, sets the table, does the dishes) and the dreamer agrees, when fearful, "I wear myself out. Then I'm even madder at my husband, because I'm tired, but now I see it's also because he reminds me so much of my alcoholic dad."

This dream reveals the way this complex grabs the client each time a similar event triggers it, and plays out all the accumulated feelings since her young childhood. No wonder there is so much emotional voltage on this issue for this client! The dream mercifully lets her see step by step how and why this emotional storm overpowers her. Together, therapist and client can now find ways to forestall the storm, and work out ways to solve the issues that trigger it.

Dreams function at all these different levels. Finding which of these ways a dream is working, what it is trying to do for the dreamer, can help open out the meaning for the dreamer, and help you, as a therapist, discern the direction this person needs to go. Without this additional help from the inner world of the client, a therapist could be dispensing generic advice, or worse, advice that fits his or her own typology or life experience, without seeing where this client's direction or personality type is fundamentally different.

Pay close attention, as well, to your own dreams about a client. These can alert you to a positive or negative countertransference getting in the way of seeing the truth. Sometimes this can alert you to an emotional overlay that makes you read this person in the light of someone else who has been or is a part of your life. The daughter you wished for, the son who pushes all your buttons, your own troubled teen years, a smothering mother, the uncle who was famous, your own lost dreams—any of the entire cast of characters that continue to live in us long after they're gone, can show up in our consulting rooms. It's important that we allow dreams about our work and our clients to show us the elements of which we are unconscious, but that are operating, nonetheless, in the energy field between us.

Chapter Eight Points to Remember:
Different Functions of Dreams

- "Each part of this dream feels like me." When a dream plays out lots of different aspects of a dilemma or complicated feeling, let the client act out or dialog with each part.
- Some dreams are simply statements of how things are right now—Jung's "just so" dream.
- Another dream might shed a new light on a situation.
- Some dreams are pure metaphor, showing the dreamer, "You know what this event or situation feels like? Like this!"
- Some dreams are compensatory to a client's prevailing attitude. Where he might be too hard on himself, saying, "I'm no good. I never do things right," the dream may show him his tender heart; he's a good person who tends to help out someone in need.
- Another dream might be complimentary to the prevailing attitude agreeing with it or with a decision just made. Particularly when a client is trying out new, healthy behavior, a dream can affirm and strengthen her new resolve.
- A dream can show "the anatomy of a complex" showing a pattern of running away from love, for example, or not trusting oneself. Sometimes the dream even shows the origin of this fear.

"It is imperative that we should not pare down the meaning of the dream to fit some narrow doctrine. . . . The dream is a little hidden door in the innermost and most secret recesses of the soul, opening into that cosmic night which was psyche long before there was any ego-consciousness.

(C.G. Jung, CW 16, par. 318;
CW 10 par. 304)

Chapter 9

Dreaming the Dream Forward

OME DREAMS FAIRLY CRY OUT to be continued. "Why did you do that!" might be a normal response to a dream figure after a dream that leaves you shaken when you wake. Breathing hard, righteously angry, or confused, you want to say something to the character that caused you so much trouble in the dream. A dialogue that is continued after waking from a dream, either immediately after or when you have time during the day, has been called "Active Imagination" by Carl Jung. He considered it a powerful source of coming to know ourselves and of integrating shadow parts of ourselves we may not know exist.

Whether you are helping a client to work further on a dream or working with a dream of your own, it is important to know these basic facts about this powerful integrative tool. It's also important to not assign a client to this imaginal work if you yourself have not had some experience with it. The power of the unconscious will be readily apparent to you once you experience the way a dream or fantasy figure's answers come back autonomously when you fully engage with it. It takes experimenting with these dialogs or art forms several times before you grow more natural and allow the figure to "have a voice of its own." Be aware of this powerful current also when working with a client. Do not suggest active imagination to anyone whose ego is not sturdy, who has a hard time functioning in the external world, especially those who are sometimes confused as to whether something happened in "reality" or within their own fantasy. And, if someone who has begun this work shows signs of being overwhelmed by their own internal conflicts, stop and strengthen ego functioning instead.

Jung's theories on "psychological projection" rest on the fact that few of us know all the many sides of ourselves. We know best the "ego," a name he and Freud coined to talk about the way we think of ourselves, the cluster of attributes we would be able to tell someone "is me," and from within ourselves, recognize as "who I am." Jung used the word "Self," with a large "S" to talk about the whole of ourselves, the ego plus all the sides of ourselves that may not be part of our conscious knowledge of ourselves. He called unknown others in us, unconscious or not seen by our current ego, "shadow." By "shadow" he included sides of ourselves we don't know, habitually ignore, or don't like, or aspects we see in others and hate and deny in ourselves. "I would never do what he's doing." He included even strong positive qualities we believe exist in someone else but, though the potential might be there, don't see in ourselves.

Sometimes through cultural, regional, or family "training," we've been taught to not like our "weepy side" or our "brainiac side." Or we've been taught our passion for art, music, or science is showy and been made to feel stupid for "exhibiting" our gifts. When we see these sides of other people, we may find ourselves feeling the same way against them as we were taught to deride these parts of ourselves. Or we could have a strong sense of jealousy or envy when we see someone having free use of their talents where ours were "trained away from us." Exploring these feelings when seen in dreams, or in the people we encounter in life, may bring us back to owning what we've lost and retrieving it for our lives.

For what is unknown in us is first projected out. That is, we first recognize it as "other," as "not I," in someone else. Other people may see that what we are railing about in someone else is a trait we have ourselves, but often we are, as the popular saying goes, "the last to know." So there are two good ways to recognize, or begin to own, our own shadow. One is to see what draws our fire in other people. What is it we just can't stand in our coworkers, friends, acquaintances, family members? Why does it bother us? After all, countless other people we see everyday escape our no-tice—why so much heat around this person, this quality, this tem-perament, this way of being? Exploring this can help to ease some of the sharpness of feeling, as we see it as a human quality, and a door to discovering the many sides of ourselves. Welcome to your shadow. This is called, in Jung's language, "withdrawing the pro-jection."

The anger and disappointment we project outward is really against someone like that in ourselves, or envy or sadness at being unable to live a talent we then resent in them. Our qualities and characteristics may not be as intense or pronounced as this per-son's, but "close enough" to get under our skin. Taking the time to recognize where we might be similar can help a great deal in starting to feel even a little empathy or compassion for someone saddled by this same prickly or domineering or crabby aspect of him/herself. "It's not easy being me," sings one of the current songs, and it's true. Carrying around all the contradictory parts of ourselves can be on some days a real burden. This knowledge can be the door not only to understanding the other person, but com-passion for yourself. This is the path to integration.

So everyday projection and exploring the feelings it generates is one way to pull back or discover aspects of ourselves of which we've been unaware. Dreams are the other certain source of discovering the other within the Self. And "active imagination" is one of the best methods for actually getting to know these other sides of ourselves. Very often a person in a dream who is the same sex as the dreamer will show us this other side. The dream character can show up as someone we already know, a person in our life, or someone we've never seen before. By free associating off this figure, we begin to see what he or she is like, and what feelings crop up in regard to her or him. Where would you meet such a guy or woman? Where would he/she work, hang out, how would she/he sound, what mood is she/he in? Let yourself build up a back-story.

Now enter the conversation, saying what you'd want to say to him or her. You can write the dialog down as it goes, or watch the visualized scene and then write a summary of what happened. In either case, you will find yourself having moved the dream forward. You may find yourself with some feelings different from those you felt when the dream ended. You may want to make a date with the dream character to meet and talk again. Sometimes it takes repeated conversations with the dream figure to feel you've been understood, or to feel you're getting to understand where the other is coming from. Don't be surprised if the discussion is hot and sometimes even upsetting. For this reason, find a quiet place and quieter time of day to work on an active imagination. Never start one when you are driving, for example. The distraction is very like being on an extended conversation on a cell phone, and can have all the emotional components of being upset with a friend or spouse.

This is the way Dr. Jung described the uses of this kind of discussion with a dream figure who is really an internal side of ourselves. "The unconscious contents want first of all to be seen clearly, which can only be done by giving them shape, and to be judged only when everything they have to say is tangibly present" (Par.179, "The Transcendent Function," CW 8).

He goes on to say, "Often it is necessary to clarify a vague content by giving it visible form. This can be done by drawing, painting or modeling. Often the hands know how to solve a riddle with which the intellect has wrestled in vain. By shaping it, one goes on dreaming the dream in greater detail in the waking state" (Par.180).

His way of working does not necessarily have to start with a dream or dialog with a dream figure. He counsels, when you feel a strong feeling, or a vague feeling you can't identify ("I'm feeling so restless and dissatisfied, but I don't know why"), to sit down quietly and focus on the feeling. Let the fantasies which come up around the feeling play out in your mind. See who shows up. Say something to this person, let yourself hear what they will say back. Continue the dialog. When it feels finished (don't go beyond twenty minutes to half an hour), stop, and stop if you feel overwhelmed. Write down what you just experienced, or paint the feelings; find some way to fix them into conscious reality. An older male training analyst I once consulted had four crewel embroideries on the wall he had sewn, marking favorite dreams and active imaginations over the years. Only he knew what they meant, but he kept them near to remind himself of the experience each had been. Jung's *Red Book* is full of dialogues with wisdom figures he discovered through active imagination, which he also called "The Transcendent Function," because it would take an experience of feeling conflicted, torn between two opposites, and provide a symbol which combined them both into a third thing, previously undiscovered.

One of the rules of this kind of inner work is that neither side must dominate. For example, if the unconscious insists on its way and you feel bullied by it and cannot "talk back" or maintain a standpoint in which to make your own case, stop and get some help. It's important to find out why you feel so bullied by this dream figure. Is its "voice" familiar? Does it sound like someone you know? Or is it an inner critic you always feel wins every argument? This feeling points to an important piece of work that needs to be done to reclaim your sense of your life as your own.

This may be an "introjected" voice from the past that you still feel you have to obey. Freud calls this the superego. It may be the voice of conscience, but when it is overharsh, it has added elements from the past when we were too young to distinguish the truth from our fears of punishment or reprisal. And this voice now holds only part of the story. Part of growing into our own person is to find our own beliefs and standpoints, or to make our own the values we were taught. An adult's inner voice, the voice of the guiding "Self" is the more mature voice, entreating us to see the other sides of the story, the other sides of our own many-sided self. Dreams come from this place.

Likewise, the ego should not monopolize the conversation either. One way that can happen is if we simply feel so stupid "talking to ourselves" that we belittle the whole process, making fun of ourselves for engaging in a discussion with a figure from a dream. "It's only a dream," we tell ourselves, ignoring the other side of ourselves it is bringing to us. So this kind of inner integrative work can only happen if neither side is allowed to bully or dominate.

Several Jungian authors have talked at some length about the process, the "how to" of active imagination. Jung's foundational ideas about the process, as well as his story about the way he came to discover such a technique in his own life, have been gathered together by Jungian analyst, Joan Choderow, in the book titled simply *Jung on Active Imagination* (Princeton University

Press, 1997). Jung's autobiography, *Memories, Dreams, Reflections,* written in his eighties, relates the background to his discovery of the technique in a period of his own great need and consequent self-reflection. And in several places in his *Collected Works,* Jung gives hints as to how he himself encountered dream figures and his own dialogs with them. The *Red Book,* published in 2009, is a red-leather-bound book of these dialogues as well as the stunning, colorful paintings he made to give voice to what was happening within during many years of doing active imagination.

Across the world there are now countless ordinary people who keep a written journal, journal their dreams, write dialogs with some of the figures from these dreams, paint the feelings that came out of their dreams or events from their daily lives, keep an art or visual journal allowing all their feelings to surface and be acknowledged, make clay or paper-maché figures, create imaginal worlds in sand trays or sand boxes, dance or make music to express the inexpressible. This work of translating our untranslatable portions of ourselves has a kind of sacred quality, and a social value about which Jung also talked about. "In the last analysis, what is the fate of great nations but a summation of the psychic changes in individuals?"

What we now know in this twenty-first century is that whatever one person does to withdraw negative projections about "the other" directly affects his/her social group. Wherever negative projections are allowed to single out someone or one group of people as the hated other, unrest, scapegoating, and treacherous undermining happen until peace is lost in small groups, families, nations, and countries. As we work with the figures in our dreams, we are sorting out and getting to know what we would, without this work, project as "other," "not I" unto other people. In the process we are also healing the splits we carry within ourselves.

In conclusion, "inner work," as understood by Carl Jung and post-Jungians writing in our time, includes discovering one's own "typology" with its gifts and biases, finding what one has learned to belittle, hate, deny or cover up in oneself ("shadow qualities") and bringing those qualities back into one's acknowledged sense of self, finding the motors that drive one's behavior and the triggers that set them off ("complexes"), the self-defeating patterns which block forward movement and repeat themselves endlessly ("repetition compulsion") and finding one's way to connection to the deep Self and the God image within. This whole task Jung named the task of "individuation." It is a deep and sacred work, very different from "individualism," which takes the easy way out, and settles for short term satisfaction, "what feels good at the moment."

Dreams are the door we can enter to begin to find the other sides of ourselves, the way we perceive the world, and the hidden inner fountain that gives us life. Active imagination is the technique of dreaming this dream forward.

It is an exciting dialogue which surprises us over and over. There is indeed more to ourselves and the inner world than meets the eye.

Chapter Nine: Points to Remember
Dreaming the Dream Forward

- "Active Imagination" is Jung's term for dialoging in some way with the dream or an imaginal figure which comes up when you close your eyes and focus on a feeling.
- Dialoging with another side of yourself helps all of us keep from blaming someone for the hurts and unfinished business we carry inside.
- Dreams sometimes feel like they "need finishing." Try this, and see where it goes.
- When you find yourself asking or answering a dream figure, take some time to write a dialog, or visualize the dialog and then fix it into consciousness in some way.
- Some ways are:
    - *writing it in a journal or loose-leaf notebook, dating and adding further conversations with this same or other dream figures
    - *Painting the feelings or landscape or figure you met in your dialog
    - *Sculpting or modeling with clay
    - *Letting the dream or active imagination speak, "voicing" it out loud
    - *Dancing what the experience felt like
    - *Making some music
    - *Using miniatures, make a picture in a sandtray or child's sand box
    - *Make a collage or montage of magazine illustrations
- Reflect on the meaning of what you have discovered in your "active imagination." Do any changes you need or want to make come to mind? Think of ways you can have some of what your inner life is asking for. Talk to a close friend or therapist for support.

Conclusion

ORKING WITH DREAMS LENDS DEPTH and richness to therapy. You may use dreams only occasionally with some clients, while other clients may tend to bring them into sessions more often. If you find you are using dreams a lot, try to keep reading, attending workshops or even working with an experienced dream analyst on your own or clients' dreams so that you don't find yourself in an established groove, interpreting from a one-sided bias.

Many cities have a Jung center with classes, seminars, or workshops taught by Jungian analysts. The C.G. Jung page on the Internet is filled with postings for classes in different cities, articles, essays, and thought-provoking book or film reviews. You will find the Internet filled with dream information, some of it trustworthy, some of it not. Use your discerning good sense as you would with any topic on the Web.

Jungian analysts have long and rigorous training in dream analysis. Their training includes work with myths, fairy tales, and other archetypal manifestations of dream symbols and themes. If you live far from an area where classes might be held, and you feel the need for some help, check the IRSJA (Inter-Regional Society of Jungian Analysts.) Website, find the name of an analyst and see if he/she might work with you for a session or two by phone.

This dream manual is not, nor was it planned to be, an exhaustive textbook. It was meant as a guide to those therapists who, while they may be thoroughly trained in their own area of expertise, have had few or no resources given them along the way on working with their clients' dreams. Because of the current proliferation of interest in dreams, it is entirely possible that a client or two will bring you a dream and ask for help with it. It is my hope that this little manual may give you some confidence in knowing how to proceed, and some guidance in knowing when to get more help, reading or studies in order to go deeper.

Good luck on your own inner journey and sweet dreams along the way!

Suggested Reading
Some Favorite Selected Helps for Dream Work

Faraday, A. (1974) *The Dream Game*. New York: Harper & Row.
Still one of the best books for beginner, intermediate, even advanced dreamers. Light in tone and easy to read, but filled with information.

Hollis, J. (1986) *The Middle Passage: From Misery to Meaning in Midlife*. Toronto, Canada: Inner City Books.
This book is unsurpassed in making sense of midlife and its struggles, dreams and all. A good introduction to Jungian psychology, too. Check his other books, especially *Finding Meaning in the Second Half of Life*.

Johnson, R. (1986) *Inner Work: Using Dreams & Active Imagination for Personal Growth*. San Francisco: Harper & Row.
One of the only books available for teaching both dream work and how to dialog with dream characters ("active imagination"). A classic.

Mattoon, M.A. (2005) *Jung and the Human Psyche: An Understandable Introduction*. New York: Routledge.
An excellent small book showing how dream work fits into personal growth in Jung's psychology.

Mattoon, M.A. (1986) *Understanding Dreams*. Dallas, Texas: Spring.

> The author, a Jungian analyst, pulls out the main teachings on dreams from C.G. Jung's 20 volumes and explains them in one compact book.

Ronnburg, Ami and Martin, Kathleen, eds (2010) *The Book of Symbols: Reflections on Archetypal Image*. Cologne, Germany: Taschen. www.aras.org.

> Probably the best book of symbols from all over the world to be published in years. An excellent resource spanning time and cultures.

Sanford, John. (1977) *Healing and Wholeness*. New York: Paulist Press.

> This book puts together the main healing elements of dream work with many examples and a wise and simple style. "A keeper."

Whitmont, E. & Perera, S. (1989) *Dreams: A Portal to the Source*. New York: Routledge.

> One of the few books which includes chapters for clinicians on screening out who should not do dream work, which dreams show a kind of psychotic edge, etc. These two Jungian analysts give practical help to working therapists.

Appendix

Free Association Method of Working with a Dream

Date:

Title:

Strongest feeling:

This dream was basically a story about a:

who is

and ends with

What are my associations to the main people and images:

This story reminds me of :

What in my life is it like?

Crisis or climax: (most intense part of dream)

Resolution: (What happens then? How does the dream end?)

Why was I told this story? Why did I have this dream now?

Dramatic Structure of a Dream

Setting: (Where is this dream taking place?)

Characters: (Who's in the dream?)

Plot: (What's happening?)

Crisis or Climax: (most intense part of dream)

Resolution: (What happens then? How does the dream end?)

Why was I told this story? Why did I have this dream now?

Dream Function—What was this dream trying to do for me?

Date:

Title:

Theme: (On which of my continuing issues does this theme seem to be focusing?)

What's new about this dream? How is it different from similar dreams on this theme?

What is this dream trying to do for me?

- Wake me up to a feeling I didn't know I had?
- "Mirror" or show a parallel situation to what I'm going through?
- Compensate my too one-sided attitude?
- Compliment or affirm my attitude or decision or belief?
- Show how I am caught in a complex?
- Reveal the dynamics of a relationship?
- Show where I am now on a continuing issue?
- Show me where I'm beginning to change?

In a sentence or two summarize what this dream seems to be saying.

What do I need to do now?